ALMOST FIRST DOG

Published in 2009 by Stewart, Tabori & Chang
An imprint of ABRAMS

Photographs © 2009 Sharon Montrose
www.sharonmontrose.com

Text © 2009 Spencer Starr

The text of this book was composed in Georgia, Gotham,
Garamond, and Handwriting Font packs by Chank Diesel.

Dog House seals designed by Gary Kohlman

Library of Congress Cataloging-in-Publication Data
Montrose, Sharon.
Almost first dog : the secret rejected Portuguese water dog applications /
photographs by Sharon Montrose ; text by Spencer Starr.
p. cm.
ISBN 978-1-58479-845-3
1. Portuguese water dog--Pictorial works. 2. Presidents' pets--United
States--Humor. I. Starr, Spencer. II. Title.
SF429.P87M66 2009
636.73--dc22
2009030541

Stewart, Tabori & Chang books are available at special discounts when
purchased in quantity for premiums and promotions as well as fundraising
or educational use. Special editions can also be created to specification.
For details, contact specialsales@abramsbooks.com or the address below.

Designed by Sharon Montrose

Printed and bound in China
10 9 8 7 6 5 4 3 2 1

ABRAMS
THE ART OF BOOKS SINCE 1949
115 West 18th Street
New York, NY 10011
www.abramsbooks.com

ALMOST FIRST DOG

THE SECRET REJECTED PORTUGUESE WATER DOG APPLICATIONS

PHOTOGRAPHS BY
SHARON MONTROSE

TEXT BY
SPENCER STARR

Stewart, Tabori & Chang
New York

A Word from The First Dog....

THE DOG HOUSE

WASHINGTON

Hello, Bo Obama here.

Well, all I can say is that it's been a whirlwind! I'm getting used to my new digs here at 1600 Pennsylvania Avenue. My days are full with laps in the Ford Swimming Pool, playing catch in the Kennedy Garden, and sunning on the South Porch. Getting here wasn't easy, though—I did have some tough competition!

The other applicants really ran the gamut: There were certified Search and Rescue dogs; cover models; scholars; champion water dogs; and even a litter of six-week-old pups! (I still can't believe I beat out the puppies.)

So, here are the never-before-seen *rejected* Portuguese Water Dog applications. I'm humbled to have been selected from such an impressive bunch. I promise to serve the position with humility, loyalty, and lots of licks!

–First Dog, Bo Obama

Name: **KACI**   Breed: **PORTIE OF COURSE!**

Color/Coat: **BLACK LION TRIM** Age: **2 YEARS**   ☐ Male ☒ Female

Describe your best Portuguese Water Dog trait(s) and what qualifies you to be First Dog:

WELL ... I'M BEAUTIFUL!!!

I LOVE TO PLAY AND BE SASSY.

I'M AN EXCELLENT AFTERNOON NAP TAKER.

I LOVE SWIMMING (OBVIOUSLY) BUT

PREFER SWIMMING POOLS TO

SCUMMY LAKES!

THE WHITE HOUSE HAS A POOL, RIGHT?

DID I MENTION I'M BEAUTIFUL?

THE DOG HOUSE
WASHINGTON

First Dog Application

Name: Flora

Breed: Portuguese Water Dog

Color/Coat: Black Curly

Age: 7 years

☐ Male ☒ Female

Describe your best Portuguese Water Dog trait(s) and what qualifies you to be First Dog:

I'm qualified to be First Dog because I appreciate all the little things in life: walks on the beach, sunsets, picnic lunches in the park, naps in the grass, and getting my paws wet on the lakeshore.

THE DOG HOUSE
WASHINGTON

First Dog Application

Name: JoJo　　　　　　Breed: Portie

Color/Coat: Black Curly　　　Age: 6 weeks　　☒ Male　☐ Female

Describe your best Portuguese Water Dog trait(s) and what qualifies you to be First Dog:

I'll be honest.... I'm just looking to lounge around and rest. I know the White House has 132 rooms and five full-time chefs. Maybe you could just find me a room and a chef and I'll be content.

Name: **Leo**   Breed: **Portie**

Color/Coat: **Brown Wavy**   Age: **1 year**   ☒ Male   ☐ Female

Describe your best Portuguese Water Dog trait(s) and what qualifies you to be First Dog:

Look at me. ... Come on, don't I look like a teddy bear?

I've been told I'm as cuddly as a teddy bear – I can guarantee I'm as soft as one!

I'm qualified to be First Dog because I can be that furry friend, that friend you want to snuggle up with and stay in from the rain.

First Dog Application

Name: **Brinkley**　　　　Breed: **Portuguese Water Dog**

Color/Coat: **Black and White Curly**　Age: **8 years**　☒ Male　☐ Female

Describe your best Portuguese Water Dog trait(s) and what qualifies you to be First Dog:

As a representative of the *Canine World News*, I would serve the position of First Dog proudly. Additionally, I would act as a liaison between the policies of the President and his canine constituents.

Name: Truman   Breed: Portuguese Water Dog

Color/Coat: Brown & White Wavy   Age: 4 years   ☒ Male   ☐ Female

Describe your best Portuguese Water Dog trait(s) and what qualifies you to be First Dog:

I'm a good dog - really, I am. I've never been in trouble for chewing shoes ... or books ... or furniture. Serious, I never play rough.
I always remember to "do my business" outside.
I don't steal food. I love cats and squirrels.

Come on, just give me a chance, I'm a good dog.

Name: Reilly
Breed: Portuguese Water Dog

Color/Coat: Black + White Curly
Age: 5 years
☐ Male   ☒ Female

Describe your best Portuguese Water Dog trait(s) and what qualifies you to be First Dog:

I'm uniquely qualified to be First Dog
because I bring style and sophistication to
the position.

I should mention I do require a blow-dry
treatment daily — this kind of beauty doesn't
just happen by itself.

Name: ROGER   Breed: PORTUGUESE WATER DOG

Color/Coat: BROWN CURLY   Age: 3 YEARS   ☒ Male   ☐ Female

Describe your best Portuguese Water Dog trait(s) and what qualifies you to be First Dog:

I'D BE A GOOD FIRST DOG BECAUSE I'M A WATCH DOG.

I MEAN, I'M A WATER DOG FIRST, THEN I'M A WATCH DOG.

I'M KIND OF A WATER/WATCH DOG. . . . LET'S JUST CALL ME A WATCHER DOG.

THE DOG HOUSE
WASHINGTON

Name: Anya

Breed: Portuguese Water Dog

Color/Coat: Black Curly

Age: 7 yrs

☐ Male ☑ Female

Describe your best Portuguese Water Dog trait(s) and what qualifies you to be First Dog:

I'm very suited to the position of First Dog as I have been an ambassador and liaison for many years. As a diplomat for the Portuguese Water Dog Club of America, I travelled to every state in the U.S., the U.K., and many European countries as well. My mission on these goodwill tours was to educate and enlighten about Portuguese Water Dogs and the many joys dogs can bring to human lives.

Name: **Hardy**

Breed: Portuguese Water Dog

Color/Coat: Brown Curly with white chest   Age: 2 years

☒ Male   ☐ Female

Describe your best Portuguese Water Dog trait(s) and what qualifies you to be First Dog:

First Dog? Oh yeah, First Dog! I'm qualified to be First Dog because I can run real fast, I can jump super high, and I can swim for hours. Oh, also, I love to retrieve — you throw something, anything, and I'll bring it back lickity-split!

THE DOG HOUSE
WASHINGTON

First Dog Application

Name: **SADIE**   Breed: **PORTUGUESE WATER DOG**

Color/Coat: **BROWN WAVY - LION CUT**   Age: **6 EARTH MONTHS**   ☐ Male   ☒ Female

Describe your best Portuguese Water Dog trait(s) and what qualifies you to be First Dog:

PSST. . . . I'M ACTUALLY NOT A DOG. I'M AN EXTRATERRESTRIAL DESIGNED TO

LOOK LIKE A DOG. I HAIL FROM PLANET ZX432QM IN THE ANDROMEDA GALAXY.

I'M STUDYING HUMAN BEHAVIOR ON A RECONNAISSANCE MISSION THAT WILL LAST

APPROXIMATELY THIRTEEN YEARS. I WOULD LOVE TO SHARE OUR KNOWLEDGE,

CONCEPTS, AND WAY OF LIFE WITH EARTHLINGS—PARTICULARLY THE FIRST FAMILY

EARTHLINGS.

THE DOG HOUSE
WASHINGTON

First Dog Application

Name: **Jake**   Breed: **Portuguese Water Dog**

Color/Coat: **Black Curly**   Age: **6 weeks**   ☒ Male   ☐ Female

Describe your best Portuguese Water Dog trait(s) and what qualifies you to be First Dog:

I can bring my littermates with me, right?

Name: Theo

Breed: Portuguese Water Dog

Color/Coat: Black Curly

Age: 4 years

☑ Male ☐ Female

Describe your best Portuguese Water Dog trait(s) and what qualifies you to be First Dog:

I'm qualified to be First Dog because I have a strong work ethic. I was raised on a farm working with horses and livestock. And, though I'm not bred as a herder, there are some Aussies out there who'd beg to differ!

Name: Tux

Breed: Portuguese Water Dog

Color/Coat: Black Wavy

Age: 4 months   ☒ Male   ☐ Female

Describe your best Portuguese Water Dog trait(s) and what qualifies you to be First Dog:

Hey, I hear there's kids in the White House.
Kids love to play - I LOVE TO PLAY!

It's a perfect match, dontcha think?

THE DOG HOUSE
WASHINGTON

First Dog Application

Name: OLIVER

Breed: PORTUGUESE WATER DOG

Color/Coat: BLACK WAVY WITH WHITE CHEST

Age: 13 YEARS

☒ Male ☐ Female

Describe your best Portuguese Water Dog trait(s) and what qualifies you to be First Dog:

WELL, I'M QUALIFIED TO BE FIRST DOG BECAUSE I LOVE TRAVELIN'.
THERE'S NOTHIN' I LIKE MORE 'N HITTIN' THE OPEN ROAD, SMELLIN'
THE WIND, AND SEEIN' ALL THE SITES. SHOOT, I DON'T FEEL LIKE I'M
"HOME" UNLESS I'M SEEIN' A COUPLA STATES A DAY!

Name: TSUNAMI   Breed: PORTUGUESE WATER DOG

Color/Coat: BLACK/WHITE CURLY   Age: 3 YEARS   ☒ Male   ☐ Female

Describe your best Portuguese Water Dog trait(s) and what qualifies you to be First Dog:

I'M QUALIFIED TO BE FIRST DOG ON THE BASIS OF MY PUBLISHED WORKS: ON THE ROAD TO THE WHITE HOUSE, PORTUGAL TO AMERICA, THAT'S ONE WET DOG., AND, OF COURSE, UNITED STATES' TOP DOG.

Name: DAISY   Breed: PWD

Color/Coat: BLACK CURLY   Age: 2 YEARS   ☐ Male   ☒ Female

Describe your best Portuguese Water Dog trait(s) and what qualifies you to be First Dog:

FOUR WORDS:

COURIER WATER DOG EXCELLENT.

* AT 2 YEARS OLD.

First Dog Application

Name: _Friday_   Breed: _Portuguese Water Dog_

Color/Coat: _Black Improper_   Age: _10 years_   ☐ Male   ☒ Female

Describe your best Portuguese Water Dog trait(s) and what qualifies you to be First Dog:

I'm used to being the outcast. Like Rudolph and his red nose, there's me with my improper coat. Also, like Rudolph, I have special charms and abilities. Make me First Dog and I'll share all my secrets.

THE DOG HOUSE
WASHINGTON

N
—

C
—

D

AUGUSTUS WEATHERFORD III HAS MADE THE SHORTLIST FOR CONSIDERATION FOR THE POSITION OF FIRST DOG!

Washington DC, April 2, 2009–Augustus, or Gus as he's known to his inner circle, through his poise and natural leadership capabilities has made it to the final selection round to be the Number One Dog in America.

On April 3rd, Gus will be holding a press conference to field questions and release his official candidacy portrait.

Topics Augustus will cover include:

- The long walk to The White House
- Minding your Presidential P's & Q's
- Which is more stately: The Lion Cut or The Retriever Cut
- Representing Canine Kind World Wide
- Being The New Dog

THE DOG HOUSE
WASHINGTON

First Dog Application

Name: Daniel   Breed: Portuguese Water Dog

Color/Coat: Black wavy   Age: 6 weeks   ☒ Male   ☐ Female

Describe your best Portuguese Water Dog trait(s) and what qualifies you to be First Dog:

Shhhhh...don't worry, I can keep a secret.

THE DOG HOUSE
WASHINGTON

First Dog Application

Name: **CHARTER**   Breed: **PORTIE**

Color/Coat: **BLACK CURLY**   Age: **5 YEARS**   ☐ Male ☒ Female

Describe your best Portuguese Water Dog trait(s) and what qualifies you to be First Dog:

I'm qualified to be First Dog because I know rules are made to be bent.

I mean, what's the use of always being a goody-two-shoes!

PUSH THE ENVELOPE, HAVE A LITTLE FUN!

Name: **URSULA**   Breed: **PORTUGUESE WATER DOG**

Color/Coat: **BLACK WAVY**   Age: **7 YEARS**   ☐ Male   ☒ Female

Describe your best Portuguese Water Dog trait(s) and what qualifies you to be First Dog:

I'M QUALIFIED TO BE FIRST DOG BECAUSE I'VE GAINED A

CERTAIN LEVEL OF NOTORIETY AS A CANINE ART CRITIC.

I'VE BEEN INVITED TO LECTURE AT THE SORBONNE, THE

GUGGENHEIM BILBAO, AND NEW YORK'S METROPOLITAN.

I HAVE SOME WONDERFUL IDEAS FOR NEW ACQUISITIONS

TO GRACE THE HALLS OF THE WHITE HOUSE.

First Dog Application

Name: Cassie   Breed: Portuguese Water Dog

Color/Coat: White Curly   Age: 7 months   ☐ Male ☒ Female

Describe your best Portuguese Water Dog trait(s) and what qualifies you to be First Dog:

I'm qualified because I can enhance the image of the First Dog

position. As a cover model, I've been featured on:

- Dog Fancy

- Modern Dog

- Dog World

- The Bark

And, of course, the premier publication of the PWDCA, *The Courier.*

Name: _____   Breed: _____

Color/Coat: _____   Age: _____   Male   Female

Describe your best Portuguese Water Dog trait(s) and what qualifies you to be First Dog:

_____

You woke me up for this? _____

_____

_____

_____

_____

_____

_____

_____

Name: **Viva**

Breed: **PWD**

Color/Coat: **Black Curly**

Age: **9 Years**

☐ Male ☒ Female

Describe your best Portuguese Water Dog trait(s) and what qualifies you to be First Dog:

HOW WOULD YOU FEEL

ABOUT HAVING A TROPHY CASE

PACKED FULL

OF RIBBONS?

THE DOG HOUSE
WASHINGTON

First Dog Application

Name: SAL   Breed: PWD

Color/Coat: BROWN&WHITE WAVY   Age: 4 YEARS   ☒ Male   ☐ Female

Describe your best Portuguese Water Dog trait(s) and what qualifies you to be First Dog:

FIRST DOG?

LET ME ASK YOU A QUESTION:

ARE YOU FAMILIAR WITH THE TERM TOP DOG?

WHO BETTER TO BE FIRST DOG THAN THE TOP DOG?

THE DOG HOUSE
WASHINGTON

Name: **Kuma**

Breed: **Portuguese Water Dog, portie, PWD.**

Color/Coat: **Black Wavy**

Age **6 years** ☒ Male ☐ Female

Describe your best Portuguese Water Dog trait(s) and what qualifies you to be First Dog:

I'm a Portuguese Water Dog.
I'm a Portuguese Water Dog.
I'm a Portuguese Water Dog.
I'm a Portuguese Water Dog.
I'm a Portuguese Water Dog.
I'm a Portuguese Water Dog.
I'm a Portuguese Water Dog.
I'm a Portuguese Water Dog.
I'm a Portuguese Water Dog.
I'm a Portuguese Water Dog.
I'm a Portuguese Water Dog.
I'm a Portuguese Water Dog.
I'm a Portuguese Water Dog.
I'm a Portuguese Water Dog.

First Dog Application

Name: Jobim   Breed: Portuguese Water Dog

Color/Coat: Black Curly   Age: 13 Years   ☒ Male ☐ Female

Describe your best Portuguese Water Dog trait(s) and what qualifies you to be First Dog:

I have been around the block, so to speak, more than a few times! I've seen sunsets from the back of riverboats in the Mississippi. I've smelled the roses at Norwich in Connecticut. I've lapped at the runoff from Yosemite Falls at Wawona. My traveling days are a bit behind me now, but I sure would love to sit on the South Porch of the White House and reminisce.

Name: Ella

Breed: PWD

Color/Coat: Black Curly

Age: 5 years

☐ Male   ☒ Female

Describe your best Portuguese Water Dog trait(s) and what qualifies you to be First Dog:

I'm a search and rescue dog.

I have the following certifications: Canine SARTech I, II, III Area Search and Trailing; Canine Disaster; and Canine Avalanche.

In my application photo, I'm performing an underwater scent search.

Wouldn't I make an excellent addition to the First Family?

Name: **Charlie**

Breed: **Portuguese Water Dog**

Color/Coat: **Black Wavy**

Age: **6 weeks**

☒ Male ☐ Female

Describe your best Portuguese Water Dog trait(s) and what qualifies you to be First Dog:

1. Puppy Breath

2. Puppy Belly

3. Puppy Paws

THE DOG HOUSE
WASHINGTON

Name: **INDY**   Breed: **PORTIE**

Color/Coat: **BLACK WAVY** Age: **6** **YEARS** ☒ Male ☐ Female

Describe your best Portuguese Water Dog trait(s) and what qualifies you to be First Dog:

FIRST DOG... WHOA, FAR OUT.

Name: Fiona   Breed: Portuguese Water Dog

Color/Coat: Black Curly   Age: 9 years   ☐ Male   ☒ Female

Describe your best Portuguese Water Dog trait(s) and what qualifies you to be First Dog:

My education easily qualifies me to be First Dog. I have a BA from Yale, where I double-majored in Russian literature and theoretical nuclear physics and minored in French. I obtained my MA from Harvard in cultural anthropology, specializing in uncontacted South American indigenous peoples. And I'm nearing completion of my PhD at Columbia, where I've been studying journalism, with an emphasis on new media and their influence on minors.

Plus, I think I bring a unique sense of irony to the position of First Dog.

Name: **LUCY**   Breed: **PWd**

Color/Coat: **Black Wavy**   Age: **4 yeaRs**   ☐ Male ☒ Female

Describe your best Portuguese Water Dog trait(s) and what qualifies you to be First Dog:

Add a little flaiR to tHe WHite House-bRing me on as FiRst dog and sHowcase my abilities as a danceR. I'm pRoficient in BallRoom, Waltz, Salsa, and FoxtRot. I'm cuRRently bRoadening my HoRizons and leaRning some Hip-Hop, specifically popping/Locking and cRumping. Let's get buck!

THE DOG HOUSE
WASHINGTON

First Dog Application

Name: **BEGSLEY**   Breed: **PWD**

Color/Coat: **BROWN/WHITE WAVY**   Age: **4 YEARS**   ☒ Male   ☐ Female

Describe your best Portuguese Water Dog trait(s) and what qualifies you to be First Dog:

I JUST COMPLETED AN INTENSIVE OBEDIENCE AND TRAINING
COURSE AT THE EXCLUSIVE HALIFAX DOG ACADEMY IN NOVA
SCOTIA. IN ADDITION TO LEARNING ALL THE BASIC COMMANDS,
I WORKED UPWARDS OF SIX HOURS PER DAY ON CRAB BOATS — I
DEVELOPED QUITE THE TASTE FOR SNOW CRAB! HONESTLY THOUGH,
I'M JUST LOOKING FOR A LOVING FAMILY WHO IS SEEKING THE
IDEAL FAMILY DOG — ME!

THE DOG HOUSE
WASHINGTON

Name: Poseideon

Breed: Portuguese Water Dog

Color/Coat: Black&White Curly (yin/yang marking)

Age: 5 years

☒ Male ☐ Female

Describe your best Portuguese Water Dog trait(s) and what qualifies you to be First Dog:

My path has led me to become a student of Eastern philosophy. As such I bring a sense of calm to my surroundings. And, I can help to enhance the feng shui of the White House and Oval Office.

Name: **Abby**   Breed: **Portuguese Water Dog**

Color/Coat: **Black Curly**   Age: **6 weeks**   ☐ Male   ☒ Female

Describe your best Portuguese Water Dog trait(s) and what qualifies you to be First Dog:

I'm qualified to be First Dog because my littermates voted me Best Nap Taker.

Name: **Feliciana**

Breed: **Cão de Agua**

Color/Coat: **Pelo Encaracolado de preto e branco**

Age: **3 Anós**

☐ Male   ☒ Female

Describe your best Portuguese Water Dog trait(s) and what qualifies you to be First Dog:

Eu qualifited para ser primeiro cão porque eu amo a vida! Eu amo ter o divertimento e jogá-lo, andando nas madeiras, e explorar lugares novos. Se você me escolhe, eu serei seu companheiro leal para sempre.

Name: *Ginger*

Breed: *Portuguese Water Dog*

Color/Coat: *Black Wavy*

Age: *5 years*

☐ Male   ☒ Female

Describe your best Portuguese Water Dog trait(s) and what qualifies you to be First Dog:

I'm ready for my close-up, Mr. President . . .

Name: **ACE**   Breed: **PORTUGUESE WATER DOG**

Color/Coat: **BLACK WAVY**   Age: **6 YEARS**   ☒ Male   ☐ Female

Describe your best Portuguese Water Dog trait(s) and what qualifies you to be First Dog:

I'M A CERTIFIED COAST GUARD RESCUE DOG. I'VE BEEN DEPLOYED IN CRISIS SITUATIONS ALL OVER THE PACIFIC OCEAN AND IN THE ATLANTIC AT CAPE COD AND SOUTH IN NANTUCKET SOUND. I WOULD BE HAPPY TO SERVE AS THE LIFE GUARD FOR THE WHITE HOUSE POOL—IN ADDITION, OF COURSE, TO MY DUTIES AS FIRST DOG.

THE DOG HOUSE
WASHINGTON

First Dog Application

Name: **Momo**

Breed: **Portie**

Color/Coat **Black & White Curly** Age: **3 years** ☑ Male ☐ Female

Describe your best Portuguese Water Dog trait(s) and what qualifies you to be First Dog:

Mahalo!

Greetings from Punaluu.

Everything's mellow.
Make me First Dog and I'll
show you some Island Life and
Island Style. We'll sail on
a wa a kaulua and swim with
sea turtles!

Name: THOMPSON   Breed: PORTUGUESE WATER DOG

Color/Coat: BLACK WAVY   Age: 11 YEARS   ☒ Male ☐ Female

Describe your best Portuguese Water Dog trait(s) and what qualifies you to be First Dog:

I'M QUALIFIED TO BE FIRST DOG AS I'M A PERSONAL SECURITY EXPERT.

I WILL MAN (DOG) MY POST AND MAINTAIN A 50-YARD PERIMETER AROUND THE WHITE HOUSE. YOU WILL HAVE NEVER FELT MORE SECURE.

THE DOG HOUSE
WASHINGTON

First Dog Application

Name: *Harley* Breed: *Portuguese Water Dog*

Color/Coat: *Black & White Curly* Age: *4 years* ☐ Male ☑ Female

Describe your best Portuguese Water Dog trait(s) and what qualifies you to be First Dog:

I'm qualified to be First Dog because I've spent the last three years working as a social secretary. As such, my duties included scheduling social engagements, planning events, organizing luncheons and fundraisers, as well as deciding acceptable social company. I'm sure my abilities would only enhance the position of First Dog.

Name: Sophie   Breed: Portie

Color/Coat: Black Curly (lion cut)   Age: 3 years   ☐ Male   ☒ Female

Describe your best Portuguese Water Dog trait(s) and what qualifies you to be First Dog:

Well, I'm a people dog — I live for greeting guests. Imagine this: me happily galloping across the South Lawn to greet visitors and, of course, Mr. and Mrs. President whenever they return home.

THE DOG HOUSE
WASHINGTON

First Dog Application

Name: RUBY

Breed: PORTUGUESE WATER DOG

Color/Coat: BROWN WAVY

Age: 5 YEARS

☐ Male ☒ Female

Describe your best Portuguese Water Dog trait(s) and what qualifies you to be First Dog:

COMMANDS: SIT, STAY, LIE DOWN, ROLL OVER, SPEAK

SPECIAL SKILLS: "BRING ME A BEER"; "BRING ME MY SLIPPERS";
"FETCH THE PAPER"*

*I CHARGE EXTRA FOR CLIPPING OUT NEGATIVE PRESS

Name: **Flash** Breed: **Portuguese Water Dog**

Color/Coat: **Black Curly (lion cut for speed)** Age: **4 years** ☐ Male ☒ Female

Describe your best Portuguese Water Dog trait(s) and what qualifies you to be First Dog:

I'm an agility dog prized for my speed. I've won the following titles:

2008 Longbeach AKC Agility: Gamblers Individual Round 1st; Regular Round 2nd; Jumpers Individual Round 1st.

2007 NADAC Versatility medalist (Vers MEDAL) Skilled Category 2nd Overall.

P.S. Do I have to take a test for performance-enhancing substances?

Name **Rex**   Breed: **pwd**

Color/Coat: **Black Wavy**   Age: **6 weeks** ☒ Male   ☐ Female

Describe your best Portuguese Water Dog trait(s) and what qualifies you to be First Dog:

My best trait is my ability to entertain myself. Just give me some toys and a little bed, and stick me in a corner (or a curve) of the Oval Office, and I'll keep myself busy for hours.

*I do need the occasional bathroom break, though.

First Dog Application

Name: Calvin

Breed: Portuguese Water Dog

Color/Coat: Black Wavy

Age: 2 years

☒ Male ☐ Female

Describe your best Portuguese Water Dog trait(s) and what qualifies you to be First Dog:

First Dog qualifications . . . right.
Well, I'm very sweet.
I'm kind. And, um, I'm somewhat shy.

Name: LEILA   Breed: PORTUGUESE WATER DOG

Color/Coat: BLACK WAVY   Age: ONE YEAR   ☐ Male ☒ Female

Describe your best Portuguese Water Dog trait(s) and what qualifies you to be First Dog:

I'M A STUDENT OF ALL THE FAMOUS DOGS, LIKE:
RIN TIN TIN, ANDREW, LASSIE, BENJI, EDDIE,
TIGER, TRAMP, ASTA, AND, OF COURSE, SNOWY.
I'LL BRING YOU YOUR SLIPPERS AND SHOW YOU
AND THE FIRST FAMILY ENDLESS LOYALTY.

Name: **Dylan**

Breed: **Portie**

Color/Coat: **Black Curly**

Age: **7 years**

☒ Male ☐ Female

Describe your best Portuguese Water Dog trait(s) and what qualifies you to be First Dog:

My best trait is that I love to do stuff! Walking, running, playing, sniffing, barking, digging, chasing - I'm big on chasing. Squirrels, birds, cats, balls, socks - you name it. If it moves, I'll chase it! The only thing I don't like so much is sitting still. I gotta be moving, know what I mean?

Name: **WINSTON**   Breed: **PORTUGUESE WATER DOG**

Color/Coat: **BROWN CURLY**   Age: **10 YEARS**   ☒ Male   ☐ Female

Describe your best Portuguese Water Dog trait(s) and what qualifies you to be First Dog:

I'M QUALIFIED TO BE FIRST DOG BECAUSE I'M

AN EXCELLENT ALARM CLOCK. I'VE NEVER MISSED

A DAY IN TEN YEARS. 6:30 AM—SHARP.

IMAGINE WAKING UP TO THIS MUG EVERY DAY.

THE DOG HOUSE
WASHINGTON

First Dog Application

Name: Leyna   Breed: Portuguese Water Dog

Color/Coat: Curly Brown   Age: Four Years ☐ Male ☒ Female

Describe your best Portuguese Water Dog trait(s) and what qualifies you to be First Dog:

I love boats and fishing. I'm a direct descendant of Vasco Bensaude's famed founding sire and breed standard stud, Leao. I've traveled to Portugal many times and worked fishing boats along the coast from Viana do Castelo south to Lisboa.

I'm an excellent swimmer and trusted companion. I would love to sail on the First Boat-is there a Sea Farer One?

Name: **Fernando**   Breed: **Portuguese Water Dog**

Color/Coat: **Black Curly (Tuxedo)**   Age: **4 years**   ☒ Male ☐ Female

Describe your best Portuguese Water Dog trait(s) and what qualifies you to be First Dog:

I am qualified to be First Dog because I have calm energy. In fact, I'd say I'm the quintessential calm, submissive dog.

Are you ready to be my calm assertive pack leader?

Thank You....

Susan Cucura

Gary Kohlman

Rahmine Slami

Erik Hillard

Sarah Clifford

Charles Lee

www.miauhaus.com

Kristen Latta

Bob Weinberg

Betsy Amster

James Lockhart

WWW.ICONLA.COM

Jack Nitowitz & Sally Field

Terry Newgard

WWW.CITRUSHILLCANINECENTER.COM

Leslie Stoker, Galen Smith, Kate Norment and STC Staff

ALL THE ALMOST FIRST DOGS AND THEIR OWNERS

THE DOG HOUSE

WASHINGTON